The Illustrated Rules of
SOFTBALL

By Anne Sublett
Illustrated by Patrick Kelley

Davidson Titles, Inc. • Jackson, Tennessee

This book is dedicated to my mom (the best coach I ever had), my dad, my two brothers, Lauren, Emily, and Coach Walker. Their support of me during this endeavor made a dream a reality.

—A.S.

To B.V.M., all my love.

Special thanks to the Heaven's Devils softball team, and especially to Mike and Mary Jo Murphy, Michelle Murphy, Jennifer Glass, Suzy Gibson, and Maggie McGlynn.

—P.K.

First Hardcover Library Bound Edition
Published in 1996 by Davidson Titles, Inc.
101 Executive Drive, Jackson, Tennessee 38305
1-800-433-3903

Copyright © 1996 by Hambleton-Hill Publishing, Inc.

First published by Ideals Children's Books
An imprint of Hambleton-Hill Publishing, Inc.
Nashville, Tennessee 37218

Printed and bound in the United States of America

Publisher Cataloging-in-Publication Data
Sublett, Anne.
    The illustrated rules of softball / by Anne Sublett ; illustrated by Patrick Kelley.
      p.   cm.—(Illustrated Rules of the Game)
    Summary: The basic rules of softball are explained in simplified terms with full-color illustrations. Information on players' positions, officials' signals, and good sportsmanship is included.
    ISBN 1-884756-14-X
    1. Softball—Rules—Juvenile literature. [1. Softball—Rules.] I. Kelley, Patrick, ill. II. Title.
    796.357'8—dc20   1996   CIP   AC
    L.O.C. Catalog Card Number: 95-070746
    Series ISBN: 1-884756-06-9
    Series L.O.C. Catalog Card Number: 94-73903

Reviewed and endorsed by the Amateur Softball Association.

The Amateur Softball Association (ASA) is the National Governing Body (NGB) for softball, representing and directing the sport at all levels of competition from youth to the Olympic Games. The ASA has many important responsibilities as the NGB of amateur softball in the United States, including regulating competition to assure fairness and equal opportunity to the thousands of teams and umpires who play the sport. The ASA annually registers over 270,000 teams and 58,000 umpires including over 70,000 teams with players under the age of 18. The ASA also provides competition opportunities from the local league level to its 60 National Championships. In 1996, the sport of softball will also debut as a full medal sport on the program of the 1996 Olympic Games in Atlanta.

Table of Contents

Note to Parents:

The Illustrated Rules of Softball introduces young players to the basic rules of the game. Each rule is presented in a simplified form and is accompanied by detailed illustrations for added clarity. Included is the information that is thought to be of most interest to young players. The fact-filled text and informative illustrations provide a basis for discussion of the game by players, coaches, and parents.

The rules in this book were written by an experienced amateur softball umpire. The author drew not only from her own experience in the game, but also from softball tradition and widely accepted rules used in various forms by virtually all youth softball organizations.

There are two basic types of softball: slow pitch and fast pitch. In the past, slow pitch was the more popular type, but today most youth leagues play fast pitch. For this reason, most of the material in this book is about fast pitch softball.

The Game of Softball

The game of softball was developed in Chicago in 1887. In the early days, there were a variety of rules, types of equipment, and field sizes. The game was sometimes called kitten ball, mush ball, diamond ball, or playground ball as well as softball.

In 1927, a rules committee was appointed to develop and publish the first set of official softball rules. Then, in 1933, the Amateur Softball Association became the first official organization to govern softball.

The rules of softball are similar to the rules of baseball with a few important differences. In softball, the ball is larger, the playing field is smaller, the game is shorter, and the ball is pitched underhand instead of overhand.

Today millions of boys, girls, men, and women enjoy playing softball on youth, high school, college, and recreational teams. The sport continues to grow in popularity. In 1996, for the first time, softball will be played as an Olympic sport in the Summer Olympics in Atlanta, Georgia.

The Rules of the Game

Outfield

Left Field

Third Base

Rule 1: The Field of Play

The softball field is often called a **diamond** because the four bases are arranged in the shape of a diamond. The four bases are called **first base**, **second base**, **third base**, and **home plate**. The bases are 60 feet apart for a fast pitch game and 65 feet apart for slow pitch. The **infield** is the area inside the four bases. The **outfield** is the area outside the four bases.

For youth fast pitch games, the distance from **home plate** to the **outfield fence** must be at least 150 feet, but no more than 225 feet. In youth slow pitch games, the distance must be at least 150 feet, but no more than 300 feet. The distance between home plate and the **backstop** is between 25 and 30 feet. The **pitcher's plate** is 40 feet from home plate in youth fast pitch and 46 feet from home plate in youth slow pitch.

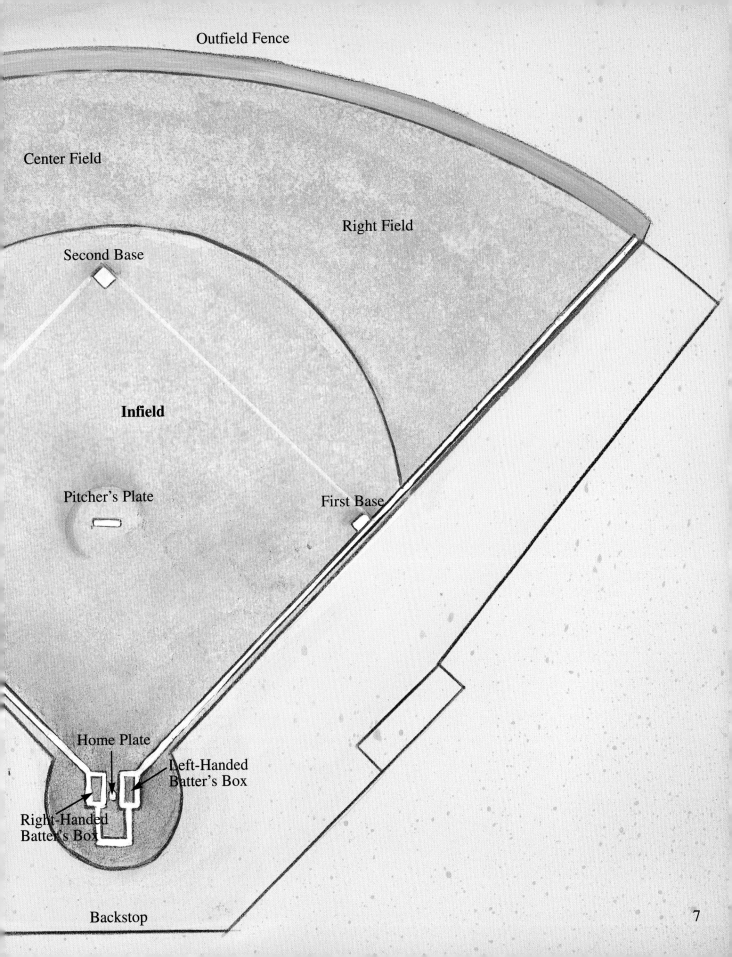

Outfield Fence

Center Field

Right Field

Second Base

Infield

Pitcher's Plate

First Base

Home Plate

Left-Handed
Batter's Box

Right-Handed
Batter's Box

Backstop

Rule 2: The Ball

A softball is about twice the size of a baseball. It weighs between 6 1/4 and 7 ounces and measures from 11 7/8 to 12 1/8 inches in **circumference** (the distance around the outside of the ball). An 11-inch softball is sometimes used in youth softball divisions. The ball is usually white in color, but it may also be optic yellow or optic orange.

Rule 3: The Bat

The softball bat is smaller in **diameter** (the distance across the end of the bat) than the baseball bat. The softball bat may be no more than 2 1/4 inches in diameter and 34 inches long. It cannot weigh more than 38 ounces. Bats are usually made of aluminum or another metal and should be marked with an approved softball stamp. This stamp means the bat meets the standards put forth by softball organizations. Bats should be inspected often for damage. A cracked, dented, or broken bat is very dangerous and cannot be used.

The **grip** is the covering on the end of the bat. It is usually made of rubber, although some players use a layer of tape. The grip should be checked regularly to make sure it is secure. A loose or damaged grip could cause the batter or another player to be hurt.

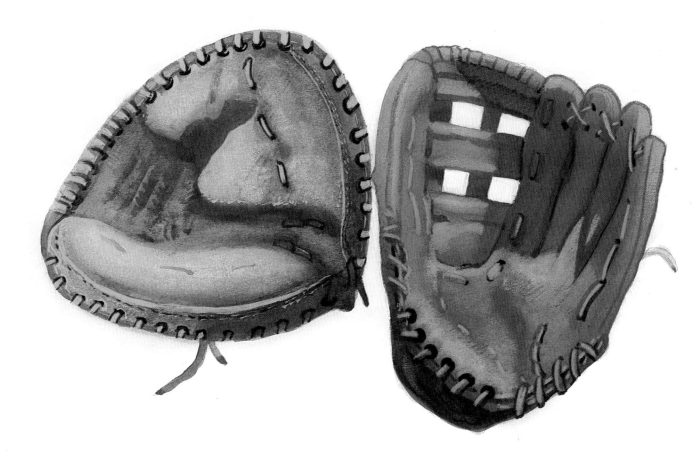

Rule 4: The Glove

A **glove** or a **mitt** must be worn by every player in the field to protect the hand when a ball is caught. A glove has a separate section for each of the five fingers, while a mitt has a thumb section and one solid section for all four fingers. A mitt also has more padding than a glove.

Only the catcher and the first baseman wear a mitt. Because these players must often catch balls that are thrown very hard, they need the extra padding to better protect their hands. All other players wear a glove. Outfielders generally wear a larger glove so that they can more easily catch fly balls and ground balls. Infielders usually wear a smaller glove that is easier to handle. Each player should select the glove that best fits his or her hand.

Rule 5: Uniforms

All players on the same team must wear uniforms of the same color and style. A uniform includes a jersey, pants or shorts, socks, stirrups or striped stockings, and a cap. Each jersey must have a different number. The uniform also includes shoes which usually have nonmetal **cleats**, or rounded spikes.

The batter must wear a batting helmet to protect his or her head from being hit by the ball. The helmet should have earflaps that cover both ears. Each base runner must also wear a helmet to protect the head from being hit by a ball or from being struck while sliding into base.

In fast pitch softball, the catcher wears special equipment. This equipment includes a head protector similar to a batting helmet, a face mask with a throat guard, a body protector, and shinguards.

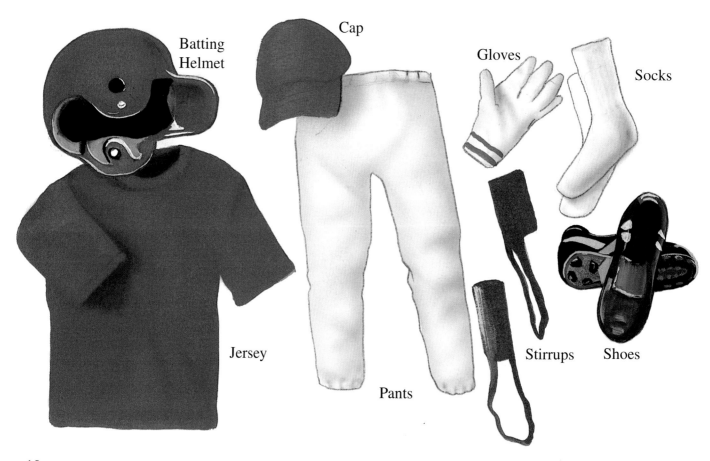

Batting Helmet

Cap

Gloves

Socks

Jersey

Pants

Stirrups

Shoes

Rule 6: Length of the Game (or Innings)

In some leagues, the softball game is played for a certain length of time, usually 1 or 1 1/2 hours. At the end of that time, the game is over and the team with the most runs (see Rule 14) wins. Most softball games, however, are played for a full seven innings.

During an **inning**, each team has a turn at bat (or to be on the offensive) and a turn to play in the field (or to be on the defensive). A team will stay at bat until three outs have been recorded. That team then goes into the field while the other team bats. After both teams have batted and made three outs, an inning is over. After seven innings are played, the team that has scored the most runs, wins the game.

If the score is tied at the end of the seventh inning, extra innings may be played. When this happens, as soon as one team is ahead at the end of an inning, that team is declared the winner.

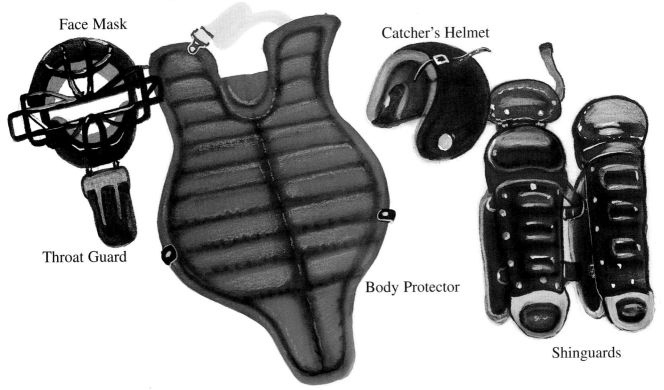

Face Mask

Catcher's Helmet

Throat Guard

Body Protector

Shinguards

Rule 7: Number of Players

There are nine players on the field in a fast pitch softball game and ten in a slow pitch game. Each player has a specific position in the field and a specific position in the batting order.

Before each game, the team's coach lists the starting players on a **lineup card**. The order in which each player is listed is the order in which he or she will bat. This is called the **batting order**. The coach also lists the defensive positions in the field for each player. Substitute players are listed on the bottom of the lineup card. They may replace the starting players in a game.

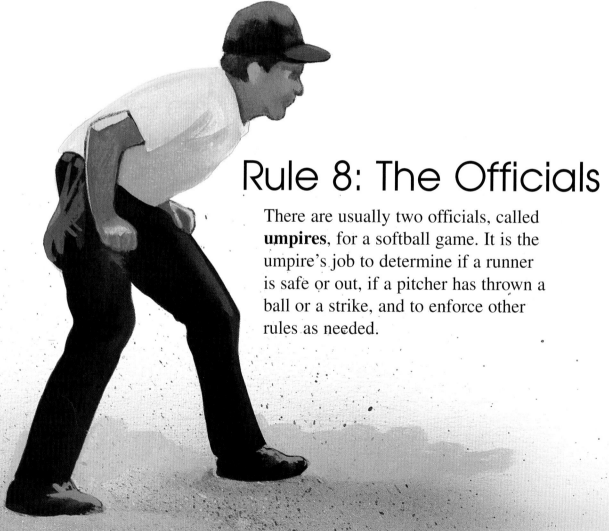

Rule 8: The Officials

There are usually two officials, called **umpires**, for a softball game. It is the umpire's job to determine if a runner is safe or out, if a pitcher has thrown a ball or a strike, and to enforce other rules as needed.

Rule 9: The Strike Zone

The **strike zone** is the imaginary area over home plate. It extends from the batter's armpits down to the top of his or her knees. The side boundaries of this zone are the edges of home plate.

If a batter does not hit a ball that is pitched through this area, it is called a **strike**. After three strikes, the batter is out (see Rule 15). If a pitched ball does not pass through the strike zone, it is called a **ball**. After four balls, the batter is awarded a **base on balls**, or a **walk**, and he or she advances to first base. Any other runners already on base also advance one base.

Strike Zone

Rule 10: The Pitch

The pitcher releases, or throws, the ball from the **pitcher's plate**. In softball the pitch is thrown underhand, while in baseball the pitch is thrown overhand. In order for the pitch to be good, or to count as a strike, the ball must pass through the strike zone (see Rule 9).

Rule 11: The Batter

The **batter** is the offensive player who tries to hit the ball with the bat. He or she stands in the **batter's box**, which is the marked area on either side of home plate. There is a right-handed batter's box and a left-handed batter's box (see page 7).

A batter's turn at bat is ended when he or she makes a hit, receives a base on balls, or has three strikes called against him or her.

Rule 12: The Base Runner

A batter becomes a **base runner** when he or she hits the ball and reaches a base before being put-out by the defense. A player who has received a base on balls is also called a base runner.

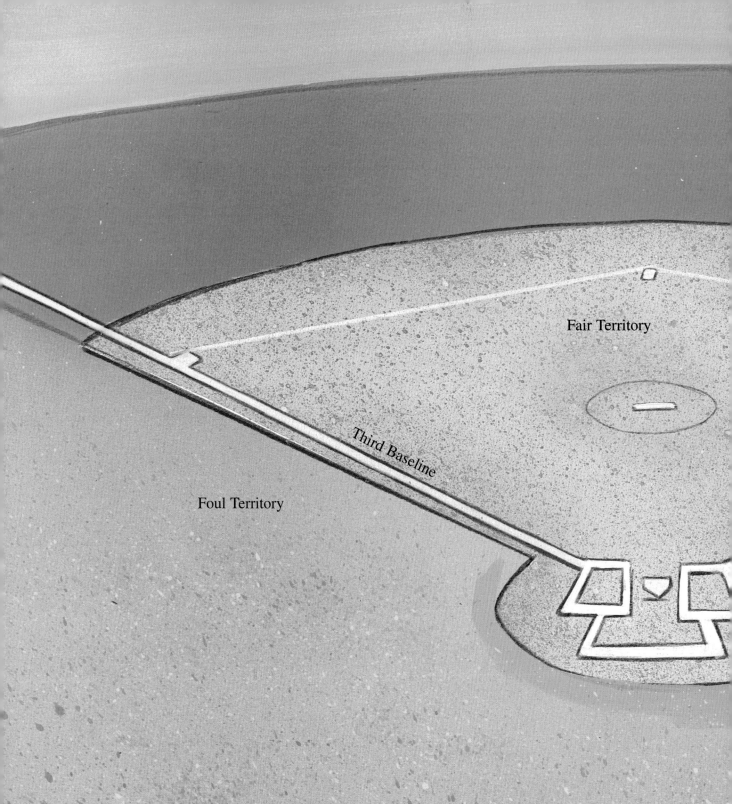

Fair Territory

Third Baseline

Foul Territory

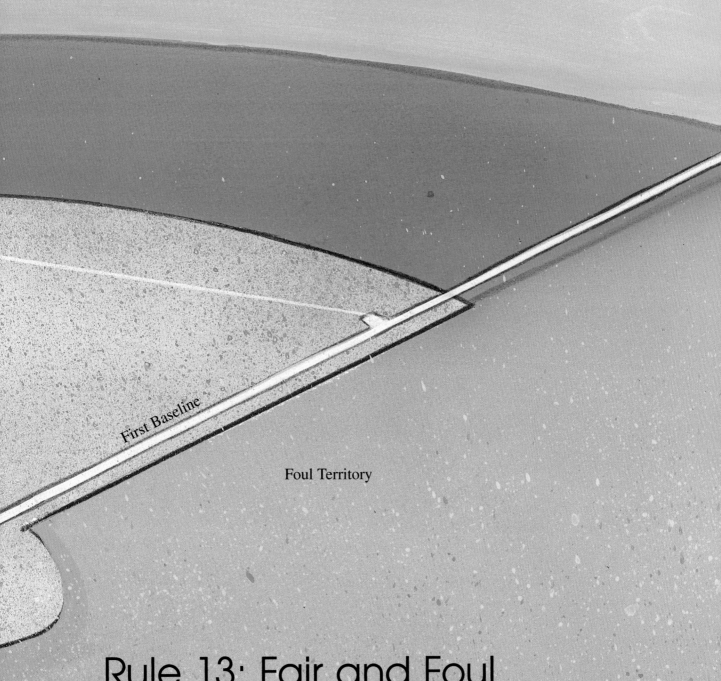

First Baseline

Foul Territory

Rule 13: Fair and Foul Territory

Fair territory is that part of the playing field within and including the first baseline and the third baseline all the way to the outfield fence. **Foul territory** is that part of the playing field outside the first and third baselines. A ball hit into foul territory is called a **foul ball**.

Rule 14: Scoring Runs

A run is scored when a base runner advances around the diamond, touching first, second, and third bases and crossing home plate before his or her team gets three outs. Each run counts as 1 point.

A hit that allows the batter to safely reach first base is called a **base hit**, or a **single**. A **double** is a hit that allows the batter to safely reach second base, and a **triple** is a hit that allows the batter to reach third base. If a fair ball goes over the outfield fence or travels far enough into the outfield to allow the batter to run the bases and safely cross home plate, it is called a **home run**.

Rule 15: Outs

The retiring of a batter or base runner is called an **out**. The offensive, or batting, team is allowed three outs in an inning. After the third out, that team goes into the field and becomes the defensive team. There are many ways the defensive team can get a batter or base runner out. The following are some of the most common types of outs.

1. A **put-out** occurs when a defensive player throws the ball to first base or any other base before a runner reaches that base.

2. If a base runner is **tagged**, or touched with the ball, before he or she reaches the base, it is called a **tag-out**.

3. If a base runner is forced to advance to the next base, and a defensive player first tags either the base runner or the base, it is called a **force-out**. A base runner is forced to advance if the batter or another base runner is running toward the base he or she is occupying.

4. A **strikeout** occurs when the pitcher throws three strikes to the batter. It is considered a strike if the batter swings at the ball and misses, or if the batter does not swing at a ball that passes through the strike zone.

5. A **fly-out** occurs when a batter hits a fly ball and a defensive player catches the ball before it lands on the ground.

Rule 16: Fast Pitch Softball vs. Slow Pitch Softball

Most of the rules and skills in slow pitch softball are the same as those in fast pitch. The following, however, are some exceptions:

1. Pitching rules: The main difference between fast pitch and slow pitch softball is in the pitching rules. In slow pitch, the pitcher must deliver the ball at a slow speed, and it must arch between 6 and 12 feet from the ground. In fast pitch, the ball is pitched straight, with no arch, and travels at a fast speed. Most fast pitch pitchers throw the ball at a speed between 30 and 60 miles per hour.

2. **Base stealing**: This is not allowed in slow pitch games. In fast pitch, the base runner may leave a base to attempt to steal the next base only after the pitcher has released the pitch.

3. **Bunting**: To bunt, the batter does not swing at the ball, but brings the bat forward gently to tap the ball into the infield. Bunting is not allowed in slow pitch, but it is allowed in fast pitch games.

4. Foul balls: In slow pitch softball, foul balls count as strikes. If a batter already has two strikes, and he or she hits a foul ball, that batter is out just as if he or she had struck out. In fast pitch games, however, the batter is allowed an unlimited number of foul balls.

5. Catcher's gear: In fast pitch games, the catcher must always wear protective equipment. In slow pitch games, protective equipment is not required.

6. Number of players: Slow pitch is played with ten players on each team instead of nine as in fast pitch. The extra player's defensive position is in the outfield. This player is called the **short fielder**.

7. Number of batters: Eleven players may bat in a slow pitch game. The eleventh batter is called an **extra player**. In fast pitch, ten players may bat, and the tenth player is called a **designated hitter**.

The Players

Center Fielder

Right Fielder

Left Fielder

Second Baseman

Shortstop

First Baseman

Third Baseman

Pitcher

Batter

Catcher

Umpire

The defensive players for fast pitch softball are the catcher, pitcher, first baseman, second baseman, third baseman, shortstop, left fielder, right fielder, and center fielder. Beginning softball players should try to play every defensive position. After playing for a few years, a player will discover which position is best suited to his or her skills.

The Catcher

The catcher is one of the most highly skilled players on a softball team. The catcher must always be alert because he or she is involved with every pitch of the game. This player must be able to react quickly to a bunt, a base-stealing attempt, and any number of other situations. Because the entire field can be seen from the catcher's position, he or she should also assist teammates in making plays.

The fast pitch catcher should be in excellent physical condition since he or she will have to move quickly while wearing protective equipment.

The Pitcher

Pitching is another highly skilled defensive position. The pitcher controls the fast pitch game with his or her ability to deliver, or throw, the ball accurately to the batter. The pitcher must always be aware of all situations on the field in order to prevent a base runner from stealing a base. Together, the pitcher and catcher are called the **battery**.

The Infielders

The infielders are the first, second, and third basemen, along with the shortstop. Infielders must be able to move and think quickly because most of the defensive plays will occur in the infield.

The first, second, and third basemen are responsible for catching any balls hit in their areas, plus covering their bases on put-outs. When a batter bunts, the first and third basemen move forward toward home plate to catch the bunt.

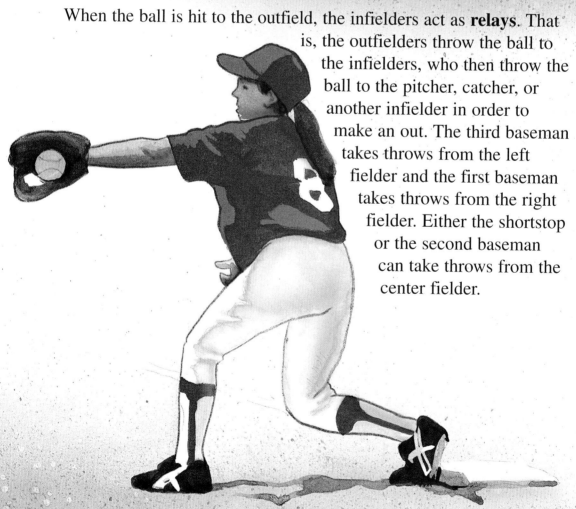

When the ball is hit to the outfield, the infielders act as **relays**. That is, the outfielders throw the ball to the infielders, who then throw the ball to the pitcher, catcher, or another infielder in order to make an out. The third baseman takes throws from the left fielder and the first baseman takes throws from the right fielder. Either the shortstop or the second baseman can take throws from the center fielder.

The Outfielders

The outfielders are the left, center, and right fielders. These three defensive players have the most ground to cover. They are responsible for catching balls hit anywhere in the outfield. They also assist the infielders by moving to back up a base if needed. The left fielder backs up the third baseman, the center fielder backs up the second baseman, and the right fielder backs up the first baseman.

Important Signals of the Game

**Obstruction
or
Interference**

Foul Tip

Fair or Foul Ball
For a fair ball, the umpire signals without saying a word; for a foul ball, the signal is made and the umpire says, "Foul ball."

Do Not Pitch

Safe

Play Ball

Out or Strike

Time Out

Sportsmanship in the Game of Softball

The game of softball is fun and exciting. It has many rules for players to learn, but the most important thing players can learn from the game is good sportsmanship. Good sportsmanship means that the players, coaches, spectators, and umpires act with respect and kindness toward one another. This includes following the rules, always trying one's best, listening to the coach and the umpires, and congratulating opponents.

Most acts of poor sportsmanship occur when someone disagrees with an umpire's call, or decision. It is important to remember that the umpire's calls are final, and everyone must accept those decisions. The coach is responsible for his or her team's behavior and may also be held accountable for the behavior of the spectators. An umpire may dismiss a coach, player, or spectator from the game for poor sportsmanship. An umpire may even end a game and declare a winner because of poor sportsmanship.

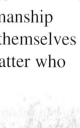

Good sportsmanship keeps the game safe and fun for everyone. Players who practice good sportsmanship will feel good about themselves and the game—no matter who has won.

Summary of the Rules of Softball

Rule 1: The Field of Play
The softball field is often called a diamond. The four bases are first base, second base, third base, and home plate. The bases are 60 feet apart for fast pitch and 65 feet apart for slow pitch.

Rule 2: The Ball
A softball weighs between 6 1/4 and 7 ounces and measures from 11 7/8 to 12 1/8 inches in circumference. It is usually white in color.

Rule 3: The Bat
The softball bat may be no more than 2 1/4 inches in diameter and no more than 34 inches long. It cannot weigh more than 38 ounces. Softball bats are usually made of aluminum or another metal.

Rule 4: The Glove
A glove or a mitt must be worn by every player in the field. A glove has a separate section for each of the five fingers, while a mitt has a thumb section and one solid section for all four fingers.

Rule 5: Uniforms
All players on the same team must wear uniforms of the same color and style. A uniform includes a jersey, pants or shorts, socks, stirrups or striped stockings, a cap, and shoes with nonmetal cleats. The batter and each base runner must wear a helmet. In fast pitch softball, the catcher must wear special equipment.

Rule 6: Length of the Game (or Innings)
Most softball games are played for a full seven innings. During an inning, each team has a turn at bat and a turn to play in the field. After both teams have batted and have made three outs, an inning is over.

Rule 7: Number of Players
There are nine players on the field in a fast pitch softball game and ten in a slow pitch game. Each player has a specific position in the field and a specific position in the batting order.

Rule 8: The Officials
There are usually two officials, called umpires, for a softball game. It is the umpire's job to determine if a runner is safe or out, if a pitcher has thrown a ball or a strike, and to enforce other rules as needed.

Rule 9: The Strike Zone
The strike zone is the imaginary area over home plate. It extends from the batter's armpits down to the top of his or her knees. If a batter does not hit a ball that is pitched through this area, it is called a strike.

Rule 10: The Pitch
The pitcher releases, or throws, the ball from the pitcher's plate. In softball, the pitch is thrown underhand. In order for the pitch to be good, the ball must pass through the strike zone.

Rule 11: The Batter
The batter is the player who tries to hit the ball with the bat. He or she stands in the batter's box, which is the area around home plate. The batter's turn ends when he or she makes a hit, receives a base on balls, or gets three strikes.

Rule 12: The Base Runner
A batter becomes a base runner when he or she hits the ball and reaches a base before being put out by the defense. A player who has received a base on balls is also called a base runner.

Rule 13: Fair and Foul Territory
Fair territory is that part of the playing field within and including the first baseline and the third baseline all the way to the outfield fence. Foul territory is that part of the playing field outside the first and third baselines.

Rule 14: Scoring Runs
A run is scored when a base runner advances around the diamond, touching first, second, and third bases and crossing home plate. Each run counts as one point.

Rule 15: Outs
The retiring of a batter is called an out. There are many ways the defensive team can get a batter or base runner out, including put-out, force-out, tag-out, strikeout, and fly-out.

Rule 16: Fast Pitch vs. Slow Pitch
Most of the rules and skills in slow pitch softball are the same as those in fast pitch. There are some differences in pitching rules, bunting, base stealing, foul balls, catcher's gear, number of players, and number of batters.

Vocabulary of the Game

base stealing: an attempt by a base runner to advance to the next base before a batter hits the ball

defense: the team playing in the field which tries to get the offense out and to prevent the offense from scoring runs

fair ball: a batted ball that lands inside the foul lines

fly ball: a batted ball that rises high in the air

foul ball: a batted ball that lands outside the foul lines

foul tip: a batted ball that goes directly back into the catcher's mitt

ground ball: a batted ball that travels on the ground

inning: a period in softball in which each team takes a turn at bat and a turn in the field

line drive: a batted ball which travels just above and even with the ground

offense: the team that bats and tries to score runs before being put out by the defense

out: or **put-out**; an act by the defense to retire a batter or a runner

safe: when a batter or runner has reached the base before the ball

error: a mistake made by a player; defensive errors include overthrowing the ball, dropping the ball, or missing a catch; offensive errors include leaving the base too soon on an attempted steal or missing a base while running

obstruction: an act by the defense that hinders the progress of a batter-runner who is legally running the bases

interference: an act by an offensive player that hinders a defensive player who is attempting to make a play